Pediatric Exercise Handbook

A Developmental How-To
for Parents & Clinicians

written & compiled by:

Katlin Middleton, PT, DPT

Lauren Baker, PT, DPT, ATC, MTC

Contents

Foreword

When travelling to another country, respect, consideration, and compassion towards others is incredibly important. There are so many anecdotes involving international trips with lofty goals where, upon arrival to the mission field, ideas and interventions which seem so simple in our homes and clinics very quickly fall to pieces. Concepts of time are different. Ease of travel is difficult. Language is a barrier. Sometimes our very ideology clashes with those we are attempting to reach. The ability to adapt is vital, and the goal of creating a lasting impression during a mission trip lies so heavily on travelling and experiencing the world with an open mind as well as an open heart.

The old adage of teaching a man to fish still holds true. Stepping into a new culture for a few days or weeks does not give us permission to assume our way is superior just because it is our own. When we arrive in a new place expecting to create change and fix what we perceive as "problems," we lose sight of learning from the world around us and inspiring change by finding common ground. We are called to not only teach and share our gifts and talents, but to watch, listen, and learn from the gifts and talents of others. Interacting with honor and respect allows us to come together and experience joyful communities, mindful growth, and long lasting interpersonal connections.

As physical therapists, we occupy a unique niche in the medical field. We can be amazingly beneficial and effective in helping and teaching others in local and global settings when our gifts are utilized correctly. We are taught to be creative, empowering, educational, mindful of available resources, and to think intelligently and intuitively while being compassionate, scientific, and motivational caregivers. Physical therapists are able to be the perfect ambassadors to individuals, communities, or even another country in need, because of our insatiable drive to assist others in reaching their full potential.

Our intention in writing and compiling this handbook is to provide a written and visual manual of sample exercises and activities which can be performed with children in simple settings with little to no equipment. We fully acknowledge that, just as knowledge should be, this handbook is a work in progress. It is our sincere hope this handbook will not only be used in homes or schools, but also internationally to increase movement, improve quality of life, reach functional goals, and inspire change in others.

* * *

"If you are what you should be,
you will set the whole world ablaze."

St. Catherine of Siena

Disclaimer & Release of Liability

This handbook is intended to be a compilation of simple exercises which can be performed in the home, clinic, school, or abroad with little or no equipment. These exercises and activities can be beneficial when performed correctly to improve mobility and strength and increase a child's interaction with their daily environment while improving their functionality in the home, classroom, and world.

There are multiple adaptations and progressions for each exercise listed. Not all children will be appropriate for all exercises or all progressions. We do; however, encourage you to be creative while still being safe. Sometimes the best activity or exercise for a child does not come from a textbook, but rather an observation of that specific child exploring their world.

The contents of this handbook are provided and intended as an information resource for general knowledge only and are not to be used or relied on for any diagnostic or treatment purposes. They are not a substitute for medical advice or treatment for specific medical conditions. The information in this handbook is not intended or implied to be a substitute for professional medical advice, diagnosis, or treatment. All content, including text, images, and information, contained within this text is intended for general information purposes only.

This information is not intended to be patient education, does not create any patient-physician relationship, and should not be used as a substitute for professional diagnosis and treatment. The information should not be considered complete and should not be used in place of a visit, call, consultation, or advice of your physician or healthcare provider. We do not recommend the self-management of health problems. Information obtained by using this handbook is intended only to provide sample exercises that can be done with children; this handbook is not exhaustive and does not cover all diseases, ailments, physical conditions, or their treatment.

Please consult your physician or healthcare provider before making any healthcare decisions or for guidance about a specific medical condition. Should you have any healthcare related questions, please consult your physician or healthcare provider promptly. You should never disregard medical advice or delay seeking care because of something you have read in this handbook.

Equipment & Alternative Options

Purpose: The equipment found in this handbook was selected as a variety of adaptable and easily transportable gear small enough to fit into a duffel bag for our first mission trip to Nepal in 2016. We wanted the equipment to be useful in a gross motor sense as well as a cultural sense: no batteries, only hand operated devices for longevity, and simple equipment unlikely to break down quickly. We understand not all individuals with access to this handbook will have this equipment and have included alternative options and ideas.

Equipment List & Rationale:

- **Peanut Stability Ball with Hand Pump:** Peanut balls are a unique unstable surface which allows for increased safety and ability to control movement due to its dual sided support. A peanut ball looks like two connected exercise balls with a small dip in the middle. It is stable enough to "stand" on its own, and challenging enough to incorporate into a variety of exercises. We chose a hand pump due to the possibility electricity would be limited in the countries we visit and likely require adapters. A hand pump also allows us to deflate the peanut ball during travel and inflate easily upon arrival in country. Our 50 x 100 cm Peanut Ball was manufactured by Bintiva and was purchased from Amazon.

- **Foldable Stepstool:** A foldable stepstool is a space saver and fits into a duffel bag for international travel or storage. On our Nepal trip, the stepstool pictured was even transported by backpack on a motorcycle down the crowded streets of Kathmandu! A stepstool is functional for adults to reach high spaces as well as for gross motor strengthening for children. The foldable stepstool we purchased is 9 inches tall with a flat surface of 11.25 inches x 8.5 inches. This particular model is from Wal-Mart.

- **Sensory Balls:** Exploration of different textures is hugely important for a child's development. This set was easy to clean, colorful, and fun. The children loved them, and it was simple to integrate them into other strengthening activities. We purchased a set of six from Amazon made by the company Konig Kids.

- **Resistance Bands:** A roll of resistance bands fits easily into a duffel bag for international travel. Strengthening with bands can occur in closed kinetic chain activities (where a foot or hand is placed on the ground or an unstable object and stays in one place, such as squats), or open kinetic chain activities (where the hand, foot, or leg is the moveable component, like kicking a ball). Adding resistance to an activity can increase the challenge as well as cue certain muscles to activate more efficiently. Resistance bands are typically durable, can withstand multiple uses, and allow for creative exercises. For a pediatric population, we recommend the "red strength," and purchased TheraBand brand from Amazon in latex-free material.

Alternative Options for Exercises with Equipment:

Peanut Stability Ball with Hand Pump → Any surface with an unstable component

- **Seated Posture/Seated Marching on Peanut Stability Ball:** Sit on a chair or stepstool with a pillow underneath the child's bottom. Avoid chairs with backs, or have the child scoot forward so their back is not resting against the chair. Pillows can include patio furniture pillows, couch pillows, bedroom pillows, or a folded blanket or cloth.

- **Prone on Peanut Ball:** You can achieve a similar position by having the child prone (on their stomach) over an ottoman or on the edge of the couch by placing toys on the ground and having the child reach for them while their hips stay on the couch surface. If no couch is available, or if the child is too tall to perform this activity on the couch, you can place pillows under the child's hips to recreate the same position. The "wheelbarrow" exercise is a more advanced option and requires no equipment. To do a wheelbarrow, hold the child at their legs (above the knees for a child less advanced, or at the ankles for a child more advanced). If a child's belly falls to the floor in a "u" shape during wheelbarrow-type activities, this exercise is too advanced for them at this time.

- **Bridges on Peanut Ball:** This can be done without a ball by positioning the child on the floor, or by placing the child's upper back on a stack of pillows, ottoman, couch, or any cushioned surface off of the ground. Ideally, the surface would be in line with the child's knees when completing the bridge, but can be lower if necessary.

- **Kneeling, Half-Kneeling, and Supported Standing:** Kneeling, half-kneeling, and supported standing are more difficult with the child performing the activity on (or holding onto) an unstable surface. If an unstable surface is not available, holding onto a stable surface is a reasonable alternative. To increase the challenge while holding onto a stable piece of furniture, place a folded blanket or pillow under the child's base of support (feet or knees). You can also challenge balance by asking the child to move outside their base of support by reaching forward, to the side, or rotating towards a toy or preferred object while keeping their legs stationary.

Foldable Step Stool → any elevated surface where a child can step up or step down

- The foldable step stool provides the opportunity for the adult to get close to the child to support them on the side or at the ankle if they need it. Other options for stepping up/stepping down can include: the first step of a flight of stairs, a curb, a sturdy wooden box, a small child sized chair the child may have outgrown (like a cube chair), or stacked pillows. For safety reasons, please operate under the reasonable expectation that it is not safe for a child to step up onto a surface if you (the adult) would not step up onto it yourself.

Sensory Balls → any substance or structure with a variety of textures

- Sensory balls are multimodal in that you can address sensory exploration while also addressing lower body and core strengthening. Other ways to address sensory exploration with strengthening include placing the child in a challenging position such as an independent or supported toddler squat, half kneeling, or tall kneeling position with the sensory substance/object within reach. Alternative sensory substances/objects can include: sand, beans, grass, slimy substances like yogurt, hair gel, and shaving cream, and sticky substances like honey. The key to sensory exploration is for the child to be able to explore independently with direct contact between skin and sensory substance, typically using their feet or hands. For safety, do not allow the child to put any non-food substances in their mouth. Sensory exploration should have direct supervision from an adult closely paying attention to the task.

Resistance Bands → any weighted object or experience that allows for increased friction/resistance

- Upper extremity strengthening is important for core control, pre-writing activities, and postural support. The most important aspects of upper extremity strength include pushing and pulling. Alternative options to using resistance bands can include: pushing/pulling a laundry basket or bucket filled with objects to increase its weight or the friction it produces on the floor, pushing/pulling a wagon/stroller, or modified tug of war style game (pulling on rope). For safety, pushing/pulling activities should always be supervised closely with an adult monitoring the activity within 1-2 feet of the child.

Toddler Squat

Purpose: The toddler squat is a functional position for children between the ages of 12-18 months, and can continue to be a great playtime position after these ages. In this position, children are able to play with toys on the ground, explore their environment, and develop muscles and balance needed for standing and walking. If the child struggles with the toddler squat, staying in this assisted position while playing for one to several minutes at a time will help them develop balance and muscle endurance.

Instructions: For children who are able to move to this position without assistance, this is a great opportunity to play with or pick up objects on the floor. If the child cannot assume this position without help, position yourself behind the child with your hands on their knees and assist with supporting the child's torso and/or legs as needed. You may provide gentle downward pressure through the child's legs towards the floor while doing this as well.

Safety: If you are providing gentle downward pressure through the legs, do not press too hard. Be firm, not forceful. The child should feel secure and safe, not stuck in this position or off-balance. Certain medically complex children cannot assume this position safely. If the child is not strong enough to use their own muscles and at least help you during this activity, it may be too challenging for their current activity level. Be careful of hip and knee joints: if they do not bend enough for the child to move to this position, do not force them.

Options and Progressions:

- Place toys or other objects on the floor in front of the child for them to explore
- Have the child go on a "treasure hunt" and find and pick up hidden items
- Have the child assist in cleaning up a classroom or play area to work on bending down and standing up

Things to look for:

- Head up
- Torso upright and back straight
- Feet shoulder width apart
- Weight in heels (you or the child should be able to lift their toes without loss of balance)

Assisted or Supported Toddler Squat: Without forcing the child into position, apply gentle, firm, downward pressure to support the child.

*Independent Toddler Squat: Note now the child is balanced.
His feet are flat on the floor and he is able to explore his
environment with both hands. Compared to the child in the
previous picture, this child has his weight shifted back into
his heels, and is able to maintain the squat without support.*

Side Sitting

Purpose: Side sitting is a transitional position which allows children to move in and out of quadruped, or all fours. Side sitting allows children to have both hands free with a moderately stabilized pelvis. This increases the ease of maintaining this position and makes it easier than sitting cross-legged. It is functionally more beneficial than "w-sitting," as side sitting allows for trunk rotation and decreases the force through the limbs, potential damage to the joints and ligaments of the legs, and gross motor limitations. W-sitting is detrimental and allows the child to rely on their ligaments and bones for balance, rather than actively using their muscles. If your child typically uses a w-sit, kindly encourage them to side sit with a verbal reminder or by having them mimic you. Many children respond well to the cues, "fix your legs" or "criss-cross applesauce," as a reminder to change position. They may need consistent cues to change their position as they play and move around their environment.

Instructions: Position the child in side sitting or have them mirror you while side sitting. Have the child side sit for one to several minutes while playing a game, such as a puzzle or cars. If a child requires assistance, provide support at the hips or trunk. The child may also need assistance with weight shifting in and out of side sitting and help repositioning their arms and legs into appropriate alignment.

Safety: Any support given to a child should be firm, not forceful. Be mindful that the child may require a slow movement in order to avoid feeling scared if they are first learning this movement pattern. As the child begins to complete this movement pattern on their own, decrease the amount of assistance. Certain medically complex children cannot assume this position safely. If the child is not strong enough to use their own muscles and at least help you during this activity, it may be too challenging for their current activity level. Be careful of hip and knee joints: if they do not bend enough for the child to move to this position, do not force them.

Options and Progressions:

- Increase the length of time in side sit position and complete side sitting to both sides
- Toss a ball with the child while side sitting
- Add rotation by having the child transfer toys from one side of their body to the other using only one hand or by orienting a game or puzzle on one side of the child's body

Things to look for:

- Both legs oriented towards one side of the body
- Knees in front of hips
- Torso upright
- Pain-free

Side sitting allows the child to sit actively, utilize trunk rotation to play, use both hands to explore, and reach across their body.

W- sitting is a passive position which allows the child to rely on structures (bones, tendons, and ligaments) rather than muscles to sit. Trunk rotation is limited by leg position. W-sitting is potentially harmful for the hips and knees, and also places the child at a higher risk of losing their balance backwards and hitting their head on the floor.

Side Sit to Quadruped Transition

Purpose: As previously stated, side sitting is not only a functional position, but also a transitional position to quadruped, or all fours. Quadruped is an important position for multiple reasons including building neck, shoulder, hip, and core stability, and eventually allowing the child to begin scooting and crawling on all fours.

Instructions: Position the child in side sitting or have them mirror you while side sitting. If the child is comfortable with this position, guide them into a quadruped transition by having them reach for an object placed slightly out of reach or by providing a gentle cue with your hand position. If the child requires assistance, provide support at the hip that is on the ground and weight shift the child forward by gently lifting their hip up while guiding it forward. Go slowly: the child should stay balanced throughout the task and may need time to compensate as they move. The child may also require assistance in repositioning their hands and knees under their shoulders and hips in an appropriate width when they reach quadruped.

Safety: All support given to a child should be firm, not forceful. Be mindful the child may require a slow movement in order to avoid feeling scared and to shift their weight appropriately if they are first learning this movement pattern. As the child begins to complete this movement pattern on their own, decrease the amount of assistance. Certain medically complex children cannot assume this position safely. If the child is not strong enough to use their own muscles and at least help you during this activity, it may be too challenging for their current activity level. Be careful of hip and knee joints: if they do not bend enough for the child to move to this position, do not force them.

Options and Progressions:

- Have the child reach for a toy placed slightly out of reach
- Motivate the child to continue their forward movement after the transition with additional toy placement

Things to look for:

- Head control with a supported trunk
- Hands under shoulders and knees under hips
- Pain-free

Gently lift up the child's bottom hip and guide their hips forward to assist the child in moving to quadruped.

Quadruped Position & Quadruped with Weight Shift

Purpose: Quadruped, or all fours, is an exceptionally good functional position which allows children to increase the strength in their arms, hands, legs, and core all at the same time. It is an important position for children who are not yet crawling as well as children who are walking and could still benefit from core and extremity strengthening. If a child skipped crawling, it can have a potentially detrimental effect on their learning due to cross-body coordination and the brain pathways developing during this period of gross motor learning. It is beneficial to play crawling and quadruped games even through elementary school.

Instructions: Have the child start in an independent quadruped position. If they require assistance, see the Options and Progressions section below. When the child is in quadruped, have them rock forward/backward mirroring your movement pattern or by reaching forward for a toy just outside the length of their arm fully extended. The child may need to be supported under the hips.

Safety: It is important to have the knees directly under the hips and the hands directly under the shoulders initially. The child may also require cueing at their abdomen as their back may arch or sag when the abdominal muscles are tired or not engaged. Certain medically complex children cannot assume this position safely. If the child is not strong enough to use their own muscles and at least help you during this activity, it may be too challenging for their current activity level. Be careful of hip and knee joints: if they do not bend enough for the child to move to this position, do not force them.

Options and Progressions:

- If the child cannot assume this position without help, position yourself behind the child with your hands on their hips and assist with supporting the child's torso and/or legs as needed. You can also prop the child on a stack of pillows to support their core.
- Place toys or other objects on the floor in front of the child for them to explore
- Place a mirror underneath the child, especially if the child is visually impaired
- Have a child crawl through a tunnel or underneath an object to gather pieces or toys before free play

Things to look for:

- The child should be able to control their head to look forward, up, down, and side to side. If their head is hanging down, unsupported, this is not a safe position for them.
- The child's back should be flat and supported by their core muscles, not arched or drooping.
- Straight alignment: knees aligned under hips, hands aligned under shoulders

If the child is challenged by supporting their own bodyweight, you can give gentle support under the hip bones and/or chest, as shown. Do not put pressure on the child's stomach as this will be uncomfortable for them.

Posture

Purpose: Good posture is always important for children and adults. With proper posture, our low backs and necks are protected, and we are able to look around our environment with less pressure on the bones, ligaments, and discs in our spines. Sitting up straight activates muscles in the back and core and is a safe, active position.

Instructions: Encourage the child to sit with "ears over shoulders over hips." If the child is sitting in a chair, you can roll up a small towel and place it behind their back to assist with upright posture.

Safety: Make sure the feet are flat on the ground, the knees are above the toes (not too far forward or back), and the hips are in alignment with the shoulders and ears. If you are doing this activity on a ball, as shown in the picture, make sure to guard the ball from rolling too far forward, backward, or to the side. Placing one hand gently at the child's back, or close to their back, as well as one hand on the ball is an option for more support. You can also hold onto the child's hips with both hands to provide even more support.

Options and Progressions:

- Have the child maintain this position on a chair
- Have the child maintain this position on a ball
- Have the child bounce or reach for toys to shift their balance and use postural muscles

Poor posture: note the forward head, rounded shoulders, and slouched lower back

Corrected posture: ears aligned over shoulders over hips

Seated Reaching

Purpose: While reaching for an object may appear like a simple task, there are many adjustments your body makes to compensate for the movement. Seated reaching, especially on an unstable surface, challenges balance and postural muscles and can be a very functional game. The term "base of support" referenced later in this section refers to the area under your feet or seat touching a surface, such as the ground or a chair. When reaching outside the base of support to challenge balance, the trunk will shift and the rest of the body will compensate to avoid a fall.

Instructions: Encourage the child begin seated with "ears over shoulders over hips." If the child is sitting in a chair, you can roll up a small towel and place it behind their back to assist with upright posture. Ask the child to reach forward or at an angle to the side to challenge balance. The further the child reaches outside of their seated base of support, the more difficult the exercise will be.

Safety: Make sure the feet are flat on the ground, the knees are above the toes (not too far forward or back), and the hips are in alignment with the shoulders and ears. If you are doing this activity on a ball, make sure to guard the ball from rolling too far forward, backward, or to the side.

Placing one hand gently at the child's back, or close to their back, as well as one hand on the ball is an option for more support. You can also hold onto the child's hips to provide even more support.

Options and Progressions:

- Have the child reach for an object or ball while seated in a chair
- Have the child bounce or reach for toys to shift their balance and use postural muscles while on the ball
- Increase the difficulty by having the child reach in a diagonal direction up, down, or across their body, as shown

If needed, stabilize at the child's waist to reduce fall risk.

19

Seated Trunk Rotation

Purpose: Trunk rotation is important to allow children to reach across their body, grab an object, and look over their shoulder, or behind them. It also increases core strength and mobility.

Equipment: Seated trunk rotation can be done on a variety of surfaces, such as the ground, a stepstool, or a peanut stability ball.

Instructions: Have the child sit on a stool or the ground. Put an object to one side of the child or hold a toy in your hand. Encourage the child to use their opposite hand to reach across their body for the object, while keeping their hips and trunk facing forward. Assist the child with trunk rotation by asking them to use their opposite hand, putting gentle pressure through upper back, or by carefully helping them to move their hand across their body. Some children may avoid reaching across the middle of their body. If the child is seated on the floor or a large enough surface, you can also assist them in shifting their weight onto their supporting arm to increase reaching with the other arm

Safety: Avoid this activity if children are not allowed to twist their spine due to injury or condition. Make sure to provide enough support for the child to prevent them from falling from the stool or chair by placing a hand on the child's hips for balance.

Options and Progressions:

- Pick up toy with opposite hand with support
- Pick up toy with opposite hand without support
- Holding the toy further away from the child will make this task more difficult; holding the toy closer to the child will make this task easier

Seated Marching on the Ball

Purpose: Sitting on an unstable surface can improve a child's ability to sit upright, maintain balance, and increase core strength. This will also allow a child to use the ball's surface in a way that increases posture and enhances hip stability.

Instruction: Have the child sit on a ball with their legs on the ground and their knees flexed at 90 degrees. The child should have good posture: encourage them to sit "ears over shoulders over hips." If the child's legs do not reach the ground, you may have them rest their feet on your thighs or a small step or box. The child should be close to the ball with their legs touching the ball prior to sitting down.

Safety: Support should be given at the hips as the child moves from standing to sitting on the ball, and the ball should be stabilized prior to the child sitting on it. Once seated, support should be given at the hips to help maintain a seated position and the lower back to encourage upright posture. Be aware that a ball is an unstable, somewhat unpredictable surface. This activity should be done with close adult supervision. If sitting on a ball is too challenging, have the child sit on a stool, a chair without allowing their back to touch, or the edge of a couch.

Options and Progressions:

- Have the child sit with upright posture for 2-5 minutes
- Ask the child to throw and catch a ball or object while seated on the ball
- Bounce on the ball
- Have the child draw circles with their bottom clockwise and counterclockwise
- Arch back and round back to work on core muscles and muscle control
- Have child march while sitting on the ball by having them pick up one foot and then put it down, alternating back and forth
- Have the child to move from sitting on the ball to standing, and then have them sit back down. Repeat multiple times for strengthening.

Prone on the Ball

Purpose: Prone, or on the stomach, positioning is beneficial in strengthening the child's neck, back, core, and legs, or, more specifically, the muscles used to keep the trunk and head upright while sitting, standing, and walking.

Instructions: Have the child kneel behind the ball, and then lean forward, placing their stomach on the top of the ball and their hands on the floor in front of the ball. Assist them in rolling forward until their feet are off the ground and their arms are extended straight down from the shoulders, holding the weight of their body. The child can play in this position for several seconds or several minutes, depending upon their endurance.

Safety: The ball should stay underneath the hips and support should be given at the hips to maintain the position and control excess momentum. Encourage the child to push their arms into the ground and lift the chest, so the body is in one straight line.

Options and Progressions:

- Have the child maintain the position while picking objects up and shifting weight into one arm to put objects in a bucket or container
- Have the child put a puzzle together or play a board game while in this position
- Roll forward and backward while on the ball
- More advanced children may be able to walk out and back several arm "steps," placing more weight through their arms and challenging the core.

Starting position.

Child begins walk-out on the ball. Note how her hands are now aligned under her shoulders, rather than out in front of her body as seen in the previous picture. The child's core is engaged; her back is supported and straight.

Child reaches for toy or ball. Therapist stabilizes the child at her hips throughout the entire activity. The child's engaged core does not allow her torso to sag or drop towards the ground.

Bridges on the Ball

Purpose: This set of activities strengthens the legs, core, and gluteal muscles to help children sit upright, squat, and improve endurance.

Instructions: Have the child sit on the ball and gently scoot their feet out until the ball is resting on their upper back and their hips are hovering slightly above the ground. Feet should be hip width apart and knees should be at 90 degrees (ankles under knees). This exercise can also be done without a ball, by having the child keep their head, back, and hips flat to the ground in the starting position, and then having them lift their hips towards the ceiling before returning their hips to the floor.

Safety: Support at back and hips should be given as the child moves from sitting into bridge position to avoid loss of balance. Support should be given at hips to avoid loss of balance to the side and to encourage the child to lift their hips all the way up off the ground. Support can be given at the knees to keep them from touching each other.

Options and Progressions:

- Lift hips toward the ceiling so that the body is in one straight line and hold for several seconds or minutes
- Have the child do a bridge, and then straighten one leg while maintaining the bridge position. Have them return their foot to the floor, and then return their hips to the starting position. Repeat on the other side.
- Have the child hold a small toy or ball above their head while bridging
- Pull a piece of TheraBand apart with the arms while holding the bridge position. This is also challenging without being on the ball. The TheraBand portion of this progression is shown later in the book.
- Throw/catch a ball while holding the bridge position

Starting position. Note how the child's knees are hip width apart and her feet are pointed forward.

Note how the child's knees are now even with her hips as she rises up into the bridge. Her knees are at a 90 degree angle to her feet and the ground. Her feet are neither too far nor too close from her body, indicating a good starting position for the bridge. Her knees do not touch each other during the exercise

Kneeling

Purpose: Improving strength with kneeling positions increases stability and balance for functional movements, such as standing up from sitting on the floor or a chair, bending to tie shoes, and picking up objects from the ground. Using the ball in front of the child can help them balance while kneeling, and can provide a safe position for playing and working on strength and balance.

Instructions: Have the child put both knees on the ground and lift their bottom off of their heels by bringing their hips forward. The child should be straight up and down with ears aligned over shoulders over hips over knees.

Safety: Some children will require encouragement to keep their hips forward and their bottom off the floor due to the difficult nature of this task. If needed, compressive support can be given at the hips by placing your hands on the outside of both of the child's hip bones and gently pressing your hands together. Gently tapping on the child's bottom over the gluteal muscles with one or two fingers can encourage the child to kneel upright and engage the appropriate muscles.

Options and Progressions:

- Rest both hands on the ball to maintain a kneeling position
- Remove one hand from the ball, and use the other hand to play or throw a ball
- Roll ball gently forward and backward to increase the child's balance

Note how the child's hips are forward, her knees are under her hips, and her feet are directly behind her with no twisting at the knees.

Half-Kneeling

Purpose: Half-kneeling, or kneeling on one knee, is more difficult than kneeling on both knees. It requires more balance, and prepares the child to move to a standing position. Improving strength with half-kneeling positions increases stability and balance for functional movements, such as standing up from sitting on the floor or a chair, bending to tie shoes, and picking up objects from the ground. Using the ball in front of the child can help them balance while kneeling, and can provide a safe position for playing and working on strength and balance.

Instructions: Have the child put one foot forward with knee flexed or bent at 90 degrees while keeping their other knee on the ground. Ask the child to keep their hips pushed forward and aligned under the shoulders. This position is advanced and will likely be difficult for the child if there are any weaknesses in their trunk, legs, or if they have difficulty balancing.

Safety: Support the child's hips as needed by compressing the hips together: place your hands on the outside of the child's hips (not the thigh or lower leg), and gently press your hands together. Guide the child's hips forward. Have the child place their hands on the ball to keep their balance. Be careful to keep the ball stable during the exercise, especially if the child is unsteady.

Options and Progressions:

- Hold the position for 2-5 minutes while playing a game or incorporating movement
- Put one hand on the ball for support and throw another smaller ball with the other hand
- Transition from half kneeling to standing
- As the child becomes more advanced, transition away from using the ball for support.

Note the support from the therapist through the hips to assist with balance.

This child needs more support, and this activity is more challenging for him than the girl in the previous picture. Note how the therapist is providing gentle support at the right hip, and is also bracing under the child's left arm to give him more trunk support. Even though this task is challenging for him, the child is comfortable and relaxed, and is actively working to maintain his balance at the ball.

Supported Standing with the Ball

Purpose: This activity can increase a child's independence, strength, and balance in a standing position by using the ball to both support and challenge the child. It will also encourage weight bearing through the arms and increase body awareness.

Instructions: Have the child stand facing the ball with one or both hands on the ball for support. This can also be done with a stable object, such as a chair, couch, or short table.

Safety: Give support through the child's hips if the child needs extra support while standing. Keep the ball steady so the child does not lose their balance. Some children tend to lean heavily on the ball. If they cannot correct this, it may be an indication that the exercise is too difficult at this time.

Options and Progressions:

- Progress from two hands to one hand for support
- Have the child bend or squat to pick up a toy on the floor on either side of their body
- Move the ball gently forward, backward, or side to side to create a more challenging, dynamic activity
- Have the child walk forward while pushing the ball

In this photo, the therapist is asking the child to shift his weight from left to right. They are working on improving the child's tolerance to standing tasks with the help of the ball before attempting to push the ball while walking. The therapist's hands are on the child's hips to assist with balance and guide his weight shift from side to side.

Step Ups & Step Downs

Purpose: Step ups and step downs are an important progression in learning how to go up and down stairs. This is a skill which requires leg strength, core strength, the ability to balance on one leg, and motor planning to complete the task. Performing step ups and step downs can be used for strengthening the legs, improving balance, and making this task less intimidating when children encounter stairs and steps.

Instructions: Ask the child to place one foot flat on the step. You may support at their hips or hold one or both of their hands as needed for balance. Have the child step up and place their other foot on the same step. Again, you may need to provide additional balance for the child. Cue the child to step down. You may either ask them to use the same foot with which they stepped up, or ask them to use the other foot to step down. Alternating feet is more difficult than doing one foot at a time to step up or step down. Children will typically master using one foot at a time before graduating to alternating feet. Gently holding the stationary foot in place or tapping the foot you want them to use will encourage the child to use the correct foot.

Safety: Make sure your step is not too high for the child to safely reach, and ensure that your step will not tip as the child steps onto it. You may provide additional balance to the child by holding one or both of their hands, or supporting at the hips or small of the back.

Options and Progressions:

- Have the child step up to a table and place a toy in a bucket on the table
- Have the child bring one puzzle piece at a time to a table top, and have them assemble the puzzle while standing on the step

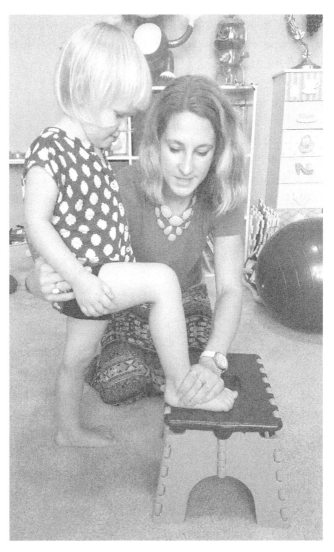

Note how the therapist supports the child's hips for balance and is assisting with proper foot placement.

As the child completes the step up, note how the therapist's hand on the child's back is ready to support her in case the child loses her balance backwards.

Again, the therapist is providing support at the hips, and is assisting with foot placement as the child steps down.

TheraBand Pulls

Purpose: Having a strong upper body is essential to complete many activities children do on a daily basis, such as sitting upright at a desk, playing with toys, and using pencils. Strength begins at the trunk and extends out to the hands as each area becomes stronger. If a child's upper body is weak, it can impact their ability to write, sit at a desk for long periods of time, or focus on school work. Strengthening the upper body through resistance training can improve the stability of the arms, improve posture, and increase a child's endurance: less energy is spent fighting gravity and more can be spent on concentrating on school work or other activities. TheraBand pulls are one of many exercises which can be performed for the upper body.

Instruction: Hold the band shoulder width apart with a closed fist. Gently pull the band apart until tension is reached and it becomes difficult to pull any further. Slowly release tension and return to the starting point. Repeat 10-30 times or 3-5 repetitions past fatigue (which may feel like burning muscles) occurring.

Safety: Inspect the TheraBand prior to activity for any holes or areas where it is thinning. If this occurs, dispose of the band immediately. Do not attempt to exercise with a band that is thinning or has holes as it can break under tension and cause injury. Be careful when releasing the band, as the tension can cause it to snap together quickly. Encourage the child to complete the activity slowly and carefully to avoid injury. You may need to adjust the tension or difficulty of the exercise by having the child move their hands closer together, shortening the length of band between them and making the exercise more difficult. Conversely, placing their hands further apart to increase the amount of band between their hands will make the exercise easier.

Options and Progressions:
- Hold the band in front of the chest with thumbs up and pull apart
- Have the child sit on the ball and complete the activity
- Have the child lie in a bridge position and pull the band apart
- Other activities, such as rows, pull downs, bicep curls, and triceps extensions, can also be performed, though these are not pictured here

Note how the child maintains good posture during the movement and is able to complete her full range of motion as she pulls the band apart.

47

TheraBand Walks

Purpose: The lower body generates enough power to walk, stand, jump, and sit upright in a chair. Without strong gluteal muscles, a child is at risk for hip pain and knee pain. This can also contribute to difficulty with balance and weight bearing tasks.

Instruction: Cut and tie a piece of TheraBand in a loop equal to the hip width of the child and secure it with a tight knot. Put the band around their ankles by having them step into the band loop. The child may need additional support to keep their balance while stepping into the loop. Once the band is around their ankles, have the child separate their feet, and face sideways. Ask the child to keep facing forward while walking sideways and keeping tension on the band by taking small steps. Repeat by going back to start, while facing the same direction. Increasing the repetitions of this exercise from 10-30 steps in either direction will make it more difficult. Again, the ideas below are a very limited sample of the exercises which can be done with TheraBand for the lower body.

Safety: Inspect TheraBand prior to activity for any holes or areas where it is thinning. If this occurs, dispose of the band immediately. Do not attempt exercise with a band that is thinning or has holes as it can break under tension and cause injury. Be careful when releasing the band as tension can cause it to snap together quickly. Encourage the child to complete the activity slowly and carefully to avoid injury.

Options and Progressions:

- Sideways Walks: walk sideways facing the same direction going left and right. Keep the toes pointed forward when moving from side to side: it is easy to cheat during this exercise if the toes point out to the sides.
- Monster Walks: walk forward in a diagonal fashion
- Backwards Walks: walk backwards in a diagonal fashion

Lateral, or side steps: Keep tension on the TheraBand throughout the movement. The feet and toes are pointed to the front and not out to the side.

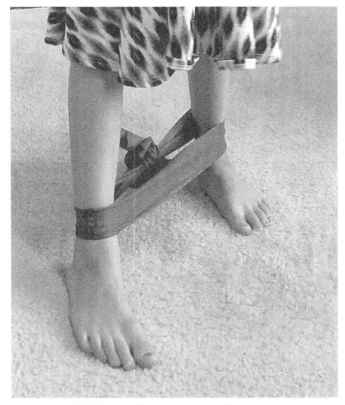

Monster Walks, or diagonal steps: Keep tension on the TheraBand throughout the movement.

Sensory Bins & Balls

Purpose: Introducing children to different textures is an important part of exploring their environment. Children can have difficulty processing textures or sensations, making it hard to tolerate different objects, foods, or places. Introducing children to various textures, such as uncooked rice or beans, sand, shaving cream, hair gel, water, silk, or sandpaper, can increase the child's tolerance to different surfaces and allow them to explore their world more comfortably and readily. At first, a child may want to avoid the textured balls, rice, or beans because the feeling is uncomfortable. As they are encouraged to use the new textures for longer periods of time, they will become accustomed to desensitizing activities.

Safety: Verify that the child is not allergic to any items you plan to use including rice, beans, or ingredients in any lotions prior to having the child begin the activity. Make sure the child's hands are clean if you are placing their hands into a bucket used by other children. The child may cry, grimace, or look uncomfortable initially; employ your best judgement on how long to encourage the child to keep their affected region engaged. Begin with shorter times, such as a minute or two, and then increase the time as the child becomes more comfortable. Do not allow the child to put any sensory object in their mouth.

Sensory tasks, especially when an object is small enough to place in the mouth and swallow, require close, undistracted adult supervision.

Options and Progressions:

- Try simple barefoot walking on different surfaces first if the child usually wears shoes and has difficulty with textures on the feet
- Have the child place their feet in a bucket of beans or rice, or walk in rice or beans without their shoes or socks to decrease toe walking
- Have the child grasp and squeeze sensory balls
- Use the sensory balls to increase coordination by throwing them into a bucket at varying distances
- Hide toys or small items in a bucket of rice or beans and have the child hunt for them
- If the child has a strong aversion to touching rice, beans, or other sensory textures, try using tweezers, spoons, toy shovels, or other utensils to allow them to play in the substance first to become more comfortable

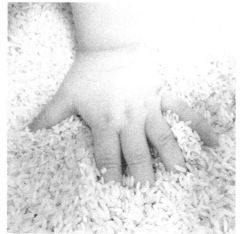

Uncooked rice.

Dried beans and star-shaped beads.

Textured balls & different grips.

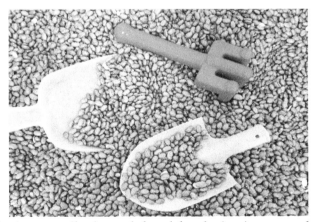

A dustpan, small rake, and shovel for playing in sensory beans.

Gross Motor Milestones

Purpose: Gross motor milestones are skills requiring whole body movement, balance, and coordination. These skills build upon each other as humans grow, muscles and bones become stronger, and movements become more complex. While gross motor milestones do provide a good prediction of development, the list below is not all-inclusive, nor is it intended to diagnose delays or issues with development. Children grow and develop at their own pace: meeting or not meeting these milestones does not automatically mean a child is advanced or delayed. If you are finding an area of concern in the following list, for example, your child does not meet multiple bullet points in their current and previous age brackets, please follow up with your child's physician.

6-8 month old child should be able to:
- Sit for 60 seconds without assistance
- Bring feet to mouth when lying on back
- Reach for toys while on stomach
- Roll from back to stomach and stomach to back
- Creep 3 feet forward on belly

9-11 month old child should be able to:

- Move to hands and knees (also called "all fours" or quadruped)
- Rock back and forth on hands and knees for 5 seconds
- Crawl (between 6-11 months)
- Use furniture to pull up to standing from kneeling
- Use furniture to walk side to side four steps
- Bend to the floor while standing to pick up a toy
- Play while standing for 3 minutes
- Walk four steps while an adult or older child holds one of their hands

12-14 month old child should be able to:

- Walk 8 feet while an adult or older child holds one of their hands
- Walk 5 steps without assistance
- Reach for a ball while sitting and roll the ball to another person
- Kneel for 5 seconds
- Throw a small ball while standing

15-17 month old child should be able to:

- Begin to go up and down stairs on hands and knees
- Lift their foot to kick a ball
- Throw overhand without losing their balance

18-23 month old child should be able to:
- Walk backwards 5 steps and sideways 10 feet
- Run forward 10 feet
- Ride on a toy with no pedals and self-propel with feet

2 year old child should be able to:
- Jump up, down, and forward
- Kick a ball 3 feet with direction
- Walk up and down stairs without a railing
- Attempt to catch a ball when it is thrown to the child

2.5 - 3 year old child should be able to:
- Walk on tiptoes for 5 feet
- Kick a ball 6 feet
- Throw a ball underhand 7 feet
- Stand on one foot for 3 seconds
- Catch a ball when it is thrown from 5 feet away
- Pedal a tricycle

3.5 - 4 year old child should be able to:
- Stand on one foot for 5 seconds
- Run with good form
- Hop forward 6 inches on one foot
- Hop 3-5 times on each foot

4.5 - 5.5 year old child should be able to:

- Perform a turning jump
- Skip for 8-10 feet
- Jump rope
- Stand on one foot for 10 seconds
- Perform 3-5 sit-ups, 8 push-ups, and 10 jumping jacks
- Bounce and catch a ball with one hand

6-7 year old child should be able to:

- Skip and gallop
- Participate in team sports
- Hop forward in a straight line

Acknowledgements

We would like to sincerely thank our parents, siblings, family, and friends for their support of our mission trip and the creation of this handbook. We are so grateful for the incredible generosity and assistance of David Edwards, Shondell Jones, and the Kinetic Therapy and Wellness, Inc staff, The Knights of Columbus of St. Ann's in Channahon, Illinois, The Knights of Columbus of Our Lady of Loretto in Jacksonville, North Carolina, HappyCakes Cupcakery, UpTown Yoga, Dr. Lisa Koperna and her colleagues at ODU Monarch Physical Therapy, our photographers and models, and all those who joined us around the globe for planning, fundraising, and encouraging us to dream larger. This trip and handbook would not be possible without your unwavering support.

About the Authors

Lauren (Frauenheim) Baker graduated from the University of St. Augustine for Health Sciences in 2013 with a Doctorate of Physical Therapy and is an alumna of the University of Iowa where she graduated with her Bachelors of Science in Athletic Training. She received her Manual Therapy Certification through the University of St. Augustine. Lauren currently works as a pediatric therapist and an online health and wellness coach, concentrating in furthering people's wellness through joy, mindset changes, and community. She enjoys hiking and adventures with her husband, seeing her family, and finding time to read a good book on the porch on a nice sunny day.

Katlin Middleton graduated from the College of Mount St. Joseph in 2011 with her Doctorate of Physical Therapy, and her Bachelors of Science in Biology in 2008. She has previously travelled to Zambia and Mexico on mission trips to share her Catholic faith, learn pediatric clinical skills, and experience new cultures. Katlin works with orthopedic, pelvic floor, and pediatric patients, and currently serves as the Therapy Director for two Virginia therapy clinics. She loves spending time with her husband and their son, reading, rock climbing, and travelling.

Katlin and Lauren would love to hear from you at EastofEdenPT@gmail.com. East of Eden Physical Therapy is also on Facebook, and a video compilation of the 2016 Nepal mission trip can be found on YouTube.

Katlin and Lauren founded East of Eden Physical Therapy as an international pediatric physical therapy grassroots initiative to teach simple, effective pediatric interventions, encourage global awareness, and provide education and care to those in need. East of Eden Physical Therapy completed an incredible mission trip to Nepal in 2016.

Katlin and Lauren worked with pediatric clients at the Nepal Disabled Welfare Center (NDWC) in Kathmandu, a boarding school for approximately 30 children with disabilities. NDWC also provides a permanent home to several of the children without families. This handbook was originally written to create a simple exercise manual for the children housed at NDWC and their caregivers. Katlin and Lauren also worked at Tashi Jampaling, a Tibetan refugee camp with limited resources outside Pokhara.

All proceeds from this handbook will fund future missions and sustain the work begun in 2016.

Made in United States
Orlando, FL
24 August 2023